My GOVERNMENT

Standing in an Ambassador's Shoes

Kate Shoup

Cavendish
Square

New York

Published in 2018 by Cavendish Square Publishing, LLC
243 5th Avenue, Suite 136, New York, NY 10016

Library of Congress Cataloging-in-Publication Data

Names: Shoup, Kate.
Title: Standing in an ambassador's shoes / Kate Shoup.
Description: New York : Cavendish Square, 2018. | Series: My government | Includes index.
Identifiers: ISBN 9781502630582 (pbk.) | ISBN 9781502630605 (library bound) |
ISBN 9781502630599 (6 pack) | ISBN 9781502630612 (ebook)
Subjects: LCSH: International relations--Juvenile literature. | Diplomacy--Juvenile literature. | Diplomats--United States.
Classification: LCC JZ1242.S47 2018 | DDC 327--dc23

Editorial Director: David McNamara
Editor: Jodyanne Benson
Copy Editor: Nathan Heidelberger
Associate Art Director: Amy Greenan
Designer: Jessica Nevins
Production Coordinator: Karol Szymczuk
Photo Research: J8 Media

Printed in the United States of America

TABLE OF CONTENTS

The United States Capitol Building

A government is an organization that runs a country, city, or other area. Without some type of government, most societies just would not work.

One main job of government is to protect people. It does this by keeping a military and providing policemen and firemen. Another main job of government is to provide services. One example is mail delivery. The government also makes roads and bridges, builds schools, and does other important things.

There are many types of government. One type is a democracy. In a democracy, the people choose their leader. The United States is an example of a democracy.

Madeleine Albright was a United States
ambassador to the United Nations.

CHAPTER ONE

What Is an Ambassador?

An **ambassador** is a person who represents his or her country's government in a foreign country. The ambassador's country is called the **sending state**. The foreign country is called the **receiving state**. Or, an ambassador might represent his or her country in an organization such as the United Nations (UN). One famous United States ambassador to the United Nations is Madeleine Albright. She served from 1993 to 1997.

An ambassador is a type of **diplomat**. A diplomat is someone who works to help his or her country to stay friendly with another country. There have been diplomats

7

ever since people in one society wanted to talk to people in another.

When one country sends an ambassador to another country, those countries have **diplomatic relations**. Two countries with diplomatic relations are the United States and France. The United States ambassador to France stands in for the United States government in France. The French ambassador to the United States stands in for the French government in the United States.

The United States has diplomatic relations with most countries in the world. A few countries do not have diplomatic relations with the United States, however. One of these countries is North Korea. The United States and North Korea do not get along.

An ambassador works in a building called an **embassy**. The United States has about 175 embassies all over the world. Lots of guards protect each embassy. No one may enter an embassy without permission—not even the police from the receiving state. The police from the

The United States embassy in France

receiving state also cannot arrest an ambassador, no matter what. This is called diplomatic immunity.

Ambassadors have the power to speak and act on behalf of their country. Often, ambassadors use these powers to make **treaties** with other countries. A treaty is an agreement between two or more countries. Another word for treaty is pact.

Ambassadors have many duties. Their most important duty is to keep peace between their country

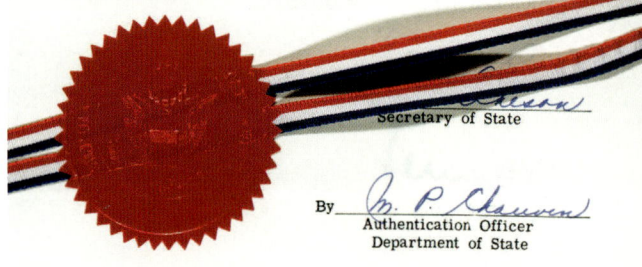

I CERTIFY THAT the foregoing is a true copy of the North Atlantic Treaty signed at Washington on April 4, 1949 in the English and French languages, the signed original of which is deposited in the archives of the Government of the United States of America.

IN TESTIMONY WHEREOF, I, DEAN ACHESON, Secretary of State of the United States of America, have hereunto caused the seal of the Department of State to be affixed and my name sub-scribed by the Authentication Officer of the said Department, at the city of Washington, in the District of Columbia, this fourth day of April, 1949.

Secretary of State

By _____
Authentication Officer
Department of State

Ambassadors help make treaties, such as this one, with other countries.

and the receiving state. Ambassadors also step in to help citizens from their country who live in or are visiting the receiving state. They also gather information about the receiving state for their government.

Many of these duties are examples of **diplomacy**. Diplomacy means talking (rather than going to war) to make decisions. Diplomacy is very important. If diplomacy between two countries fails, it often leads to war.

Serving in the Government

In the United States, ambassadors work for the State Department. This is in the executive branch of the United States government. Ambassadors report to the secretary of state, who is the head of the State Department.

Ambassadors often live in the foreign country where they serve. This means they must speak that country's language. They must also understand the country's people, culture, and customs. Otherwise, they may find it hard to carry out their duties in that country.

Several United Nations ambassadors attend a Security Council meeting.

United States ambassador to the United Nations Nikki Haley (*left*) meets with King Abdullah II of Jordan (*right*) in May 2017.

CHAPTER TWO

A Day in the Life of an Ambassador

For an ambassador, there is no typical day. An ambassador might meet with a leader or an important visitor from his or her own country. Even so, the ambassador might develop a routine of sorts. Ambassadors have the very important job of making sure that everything runs smoothly at the embassy.

MORNING

In the morning, the ambassador might eat breakfast with his or her family. Around 8:30 a.m., the ambassador usually goes to his or her office inside the embassy. When the ambassador arrives, he or she will likely check the

13

schedule for the day. After that, he or she answers emails, writes letters, or makes phone calls. If the ambassador is in a different time zone, he or she will need to make sure not to call someone at the wrong time. Ambassadors also attend a lot of meetings with top officials in the embassy to plan visits, events, and speeches.

Chauffeurs

Most ambassadors have a chauffeur. A chauffeur is someone who drives other people around. Often, ambassadors ride in limousines. An ambassador's limousine may have bulletproof windows to protect the ambassador from an attacker.

Embassy Chefs

Most embassies have their own chef. Embassy chefs are among the best chefs in the world. Sometimes, the embassy chef cooks for large parties. The chef often cooks dishes from the ambassador's home country.

Embassy chefs are among the finest chefs in the world.

AFTERNOON

For lunch, the ambassador might eat a meal cooked by the embassy chef. Or, the ambassador could leave the embassy to eat at a restaurant with a coworker or other **dignitary**. A dignitary is a person who holds a high rank or office. Afterward, the ambassador might meet with embassy workers to discuss their duties. The ambassador might also meet with visitors from the receiving state or from his or her own country. Or, the ambassador could give a speech. For example, the ambassador might speak about trade to a group of local businesspeople.

Sometimes the ambassador hosts fancy dinners at the embassy.

EVENING

In the evening, the ambassador might go to a formal dinner with other dignitaries. This dinner could be at the ambassador's embassy. If so, the ambassador acts as the host. If the dinner is somewhere else, the ambassador may be an honored guest. After dinner, the ambassador will return home to his or her family. However, the ambassador may still need to work. For example, he or she may need to catch up on emails or get ready for the next day. The ambassador will also need to be on call to answer important phone calls—even if it's the middle of the night.

CONCLUSION

The daily life of an ambassador might be different depending on which part of the world he or she works in. For example, the

Jane D. Hartley was a United States ambassador to France.

daily life of the United States ambassador to France might be different from that of the United States ambassador to Afghanistan. This is because the cultures of these two countries are quite different.

Fancy Dinners

Attending dinner gatherings with dignitaries is an important part of an ambassador's job. The ambassador must dress up, show good manners, and follow local customs at these types of events.

Secretary of State Colin Powell (*right*) swears in John D. Negroponte (*left*) as the United States ambassador to Iraq in June 2004.

CHAPTER THREE

Job Requirements

It used to be that ambassadors were part of the sending state's ruling family. That is no longer the case. In the United States, the president nominates an ambassador.

In some cases, the president will nominate a **career diplomat**. A career diplomat is someone who has worked for a long time for his or her home country's foreign service. (The United States Foreign Service is part of the State Department.) About two-thirds of all United States ambassadors are career diplomats. Usually, career diplomats have a college degree in politics, economics, or law. They may also speak more than one language. This is not required, however.

In other cases, the president will nominate a **political appointee**. Usually, this person is a friend of the president. Perhaps the appointee did the president a favor like helping with an election. Most likely, this person has not worked for his or her country's foreign service. However, there are other types of experience that could make him or her a good choice for ambassador. About one-third of all United States ambassadors are political appointees. Even though the secretary of state is the ambassador's boss, in the United States, the ambassador serves "at the pleasure of the president." That means the ambassador can be fired at any time.

In the United States, the Senate must approve each ambassador nominated by the president. This is a three-step process. First, members of the Senate interview the nominee. This is called a **congressional hearing**. During a congressional hearing, the nominee must answer questions

United States ambassador to Great Britain Matthew Winthrop Barzun [*left*], a political appointee, shakes hands with President Barack Obama [*right*] in 2014.

to prove he or she can do the job. Next, a special Senate group votes on the nominee. Finally, if the Senate group votes for the nominee, the nomination is sent to the full Senate for a vote. If more members of the Senate vote for the nominee rather than against, the nominee is appointed ambassador. However, there is one more step. The receiving state must approve the nominated ambassador.

John Kerry [*left*] and Richard Lugar [*right*] participate in a congressional hearing for the appointment of an ambassador.

When that happens, the ambassador is sworn in during a special ceremony.

Sometimes, an ambassador might leave one post only to land another. One United States ambassador named Charles Yost served as ambassador to Thailand (1946), Laos (1954–1956), Syria (1958), Morocco (1958–1961), and the United Nations (1969–1971).

Facing Dangers

Being an ambassador can be a risky job. Sometimes, ambassadors are targets of attacks. Special guards with guns protect United States ambassadors. Even that may not be enough, however. This was the case in 2012. That year, terrorists killed the United States ambassador to Libya. His name was J. Christopher Stevens. The terrorists also killed three other people. One worked for the United States Foreign Service. Two others were guards. These types of events are rare, however.

United States ambassador to Libya J. Christopher Stevens was killed by terrorists.

If you enjoy meeting people from other countries, you might like to be an ambassador.

CHAPTER FOUR

Becoming an Ambassador

You are smart. You are curious about other countries. You pay attention to the news. You like to travel. If this describes you, then you might like being an ambassador.

In the United States, there are two ways to become an ambassador. One is to become a friend of the president and a political appointee. This might be hard. The other is to become a career diplomat. This approach is more doable.

To become a career diplomat, you must join the United States Foreign Service. To do so, it helps to have

gone to college. You must also do certain steps. The first step is to pass a test. This test is called the Foreign Service Exam. To pass this test, you need a wide range of knowledge. This includes knowledge of geography, history, government, and culture. This test is very hard. Not everyone passes it the first time.

After you pass the Foreign Service Exam, you must turn in a résumé and an essay to describe yourself. Then you must take an oral test. During this test, you will be interviewed. You will also be asked to show how you would act in certain situations. This is to see how well you handle stress.

When you pass the oral test, you are sent to a doctor for a checkup. This is to show that you are physically fit for the job. You must also go through a background check. When all this is done, a group of United States Foreign Service workers will decide if you are a good fit for the United States Foreign Service. Not everyone who tries to join is allowed in.

If you join the United States Foreign Service, you must complete a training course on foreign affairs. You might also be asked to take foreign language classes or work on

United States ambassador to Japan Caroline Kennedy shakes hands with Japanese foreign minister Fumio Kishida in January 2017.

27

Model UN is a great way to learn about diplomacy.

diplomacy skills. Then you'll be sent on your first job. This job could be in any country in the world that has diplomatic relations with the United States. When that job ends, you'll be sent on another. And another. And finally, you'll have the knowledge and experience you'll need to be an ambassador. Good luck!

Get Involved!

Model United Nations (Model UN) is for middle school, high school, and college students. In Model UN, kids learn about diplomacy and foreign relations. They gain leadership skills. They also learn how to debate. This can be a great first step toward one day joining the Foreign Service. If you are passionate about serving the United States, then becoming a Foreign Service officer is a great fit for you!

Model UN
http://www.unausa.org/global-classrooms-model-un

ambassador   A person who represents his or her country's government in a foreign country.

career diplomat   A person who has risen through the ranks of his or her home country's foreign service.

congressional hearing   An interview or meeting in Congress to gather information about a topic or person.

dignitary   A person who holds a high rank or office.

diplomacy   The use of talking (rather than war) to make decisions and reach agreements.

diplomat   Someone who works to help his or her country stay friendly with another country.

diplomatic relations   Describes when one country sends an ambassador or other diplomat to another country.

embassy   The building where an ambassador works. The United States has about 175 embassies all over the world.

political appointee Someone who is appointed as an ambassador by the president, even though he or she has not worked for the United States Foreign Service.

receiving state The country where an ambassador is sent to live and work.

sending state The country that sends an ambassador to a receiving state.

treaty An agreement between two or more countries. Also called a pact.

FIND OUT MORE!

BOOKS

Armitage, Vivian. *My First Model United Nations Conference: Demystifying Model UN, One Conference at a Time.* Seattle, WA: CreateSpace Publishing, 2016.

Evans, Leah Moorefield. *Embassy Kids Coloring Book*. Seattle, WA: CreateSpace Publishing, 2015.

Thomas, Maureen. *Diplomacy Facts for Kids*. Seattle, WA: CreateSpace Publishing, 2014.

WEBSITES

Children's Etiquette Around the World
http://etiquettesurvival.com/
childrens-etiquette-around-the-world

Foreign Service Officer Careers
https://careers.state.gov/work/foreign-service/officer

National Geographic: Diplomacy
http://www.nationalgeographic.org/encyclopedia/diplomacy

MEET THE AUTHOR

Kate Shoup has written more than forty books and has edited hundreds more. When not working, Kate loves to travel, watch IndyCar racing, ski, read, and ride her motorcycle. She lives in Indianapolis with her husband, her daughter, and their dog.